Relationship Communication for Couples

The Best Help to Face Conversations and Discussions, Improving Your Social Skills and Cure Your Relationship in Marriage Maintaining Real Respect and Love

Table of Contents

Introduction

Man is a social being. Communication is probably as vital for him as breathing. The process is vital not just from the point of sharing knowledge, facts, and information, but also feelings, thoughts, and emotions. It helps people share ideas, philosophies, and concepts. It gives you access to knowledge around the world. The most important value of communication – it helps you forge meaningful social and interpersonal relationships. Society and relationships will stagnate without the tool of communication.

It isn't an overstatement to say that communication is the cornerstone of human relationships. Initially, strangers get to know one another only through communication. Then, relationships are developed and there is greater interaction, which develops into strong bonds. Communication assists us in expressing our ideas, emotions, and feelings, while also helping us understand the feelings and emotions of other people. As a consequence of this, we either develop negative or constructive emotions towards those we form intimate relationships with.

One of the biggest tools men have that differentiate them from other creatures is the power to communicate through various means. Think of it as a hammer or any other tool. It can be used for hitting a nail on the wall or as a weapon of destruction in relationships. Communication can be used positively to create more meaningful and effective interpersonal relationships or be used as a weapon of destruction to damage them.

Think of a scenario where you are upset with someone. They've been hurting you for a while, and you want them to stop without being rude or spoiling your relationship with them. How do you communicate to them that they should stop hurting you without hurting them? There are multiple ways to approach communication. You can both be completely frank and forthright and tell them like it is in which case you're ruining your chances with them or you approach the issue more diplomatically and smartly by communicating in a way that they understand without feeling offended.

Thus, communication forms the basis of interpersonal relationships that we are a part of. And knowing how to communicate with those closest to us gives us the superpower or edge to form even more meaningful, rewarding and fulfilling relationships.

This power-packed book is the ultimate communication handbook that places the tool of communication in your hand and awards you the power to form intimate relationships that others can only dream of. Remember, communication is the key, and knowing the secrets of communication can help you unlock the potential for maximizing your chances of experiencing a high sense of fulfillment and gratification in your interpersonal relationships.

Chapter One: Real-World Situations – Where Communication Goes Wrong Right and How to Tackle It

If you ask me to pick only one aspect that spells the success or failure of a relationship, I'd say communication without batting an eyelid. Today relationships crumble faster than a cookie because of a communication breakdown. Lack of communication in interpersonal relationships leads to misunderstandings, frustrations, conflict, arguments, and several other unpleasant experiences!

Here are some proven and highly effective rules for communication in relationships.

1. Use the Sandwich Technique

This is one of the most powerful methods when it comes to communicating something tricky and potentially offensive to your partner. The way it works is – you sandwich a potentially negative or offensive statement between a couple of positive statements.

For example, "Listen, Bridget, I adore you a lot and you truly make me happy. However, I am having a tough time with you working round the clock. If you would just cut down on your work, and we could spend a good time together, I'd be really happy. It feels so wonderful when I am with you." See what we did there? We used a potential conflict causing accusation (you don't spend enough time with me because of your work) between two saccharine sweet-sounding statements that are guaranteed to meet your partner's heart.

Don't throw a bomb on your partner by hurling accusations on them out of nowhere. Always use signposts or indicators that you are offering a heads-up about something so they are prepared for it rather than being thrown off guard. If you have genuine concerns that you want them to hear, begin the conversation with something like, "I want to get this off my chest" or "I could do with some reassurance that..." This way your partner realizes that you aren't really accusing him or her but just need some reassurance and hearing.

2. Reserve Important Issues for Face To Face Interaction

Make it a rule to never discuss important issues or confront your partner overcalls and texts. That's a quick and unhealthy way to deal with critical issues. Like we discussed in the earlier chapters, body language is one of the most important components of communication.

By discussing important issues over the phone or via text, you are leaving out important non-verbal signals that will facilitate more effective communication. Texts can lead to even greater confusion, misunderstanding, and frustration. Leave the important stuff for face to face communication.

Make eye contact while speaking to your partner. Don't stare continuously at them, while also demonstrating that you aren't really afraid of facing them. It is alright for the eyes to wander occasionally. However, always bring eye contact back to their faces.

Also, a relationship where you are constantly walking on eggshells is not a very healthy one. Are you able to freely express how you are feeling? You need to be able to express yourself openly, honestly, and in a straightforward manner. If you are unable to communicate openly and honestly with your partner, the relationship may be headed for trouble. Say, for instance, you aren't up for moving in together yet. You should be able to tell your partner in a frank and honest manner about not being ready for a move-in just yet. Are your needs in the bedroom being met? You should be able to discuss it in a forthright manner with your partner. Honestly and frankness is the basis of a healthy relationship.

It isn't about being brash or constantly hurting your partner with your honestly. However, you should be able to express your deepest concerns and grievances in a gentle yet frank manner without worrying about how the other person will react.

3. More "I" Less "You"

If you've ever signed up for couple therapy sessions, you'll know that therapists and counselors often insist on using more "I" and less "You" to make their statements less accusatory. "You" makes your partner more offensive, while "I" means you are putting the onus for how you feel for yourself instead of the other person. You are articulating your feelings, and not blaming the other person. For example, instead of saying, "You never help me with household work" try saying, "I feel hurt and exhausted when you don't help me with household work." How does the latter sound? Less accusatory and more open to communication and discussion. The sensitive issue becomes more approachable.

It is more effective in making the person realize that their actions aren't going down well with you rather than using accusatory or counterproductive statements that make matters worse.

4. Communication through Action

One of the most important things to understand in a relationship is that a person doesn't just communicate merely through words. They also communicate through their actions, which speak louder than words. Communicate through your actions too not just words. Demonstrate your love, concern, care, and empathy for your partner in ways other than simply speaking. Go out of the way at times to do things for them.

Show your partner that you care about them through your actions. Words have no value if they aren't backed by actions.

Tiny, thoughtful everyday actions go a long way in demonstrating your love, care, and affection. Pay attention to small gestures and details. Simply sending a "good luck" message before an important presentation or meeting can tell them you are thinking about them or care about their success. If they are worried about the health of a friend or family member, reach out to them and express concern.

Take the time and effort to understand what brings a smile to their face or what makes them happy. Demonstrate your happiness through thoughtful little gifts, words, and gestures. Pick flowers for them on your way back home from work. Get home their favorite eatables from the supermarket.

Reserve a table at their favorite eatery in town or take off with them on a surprise weekend getaway. How about tickets to watch their favorite sports team in action or a round of golf? Thinking these warm thoughts when you aren't together will show them you care.

5. Practice Active Listening

Again, communication is as much or more about listening than talking. It involves allowing your other half to know that you are 100% attentive and interested in what he or she is speaking.

It can be in the form of several verbal and non-verbal clues including eye contact, acknowledgment of what they are saying, paraphrasing what they said (to demonstrate you've been keenly listening and want to understand them correctly), and much more. Don't look at your phone or the newspaper while your partner is speaking. Let him or she knows that you have their complete attention.

Resist the urge to interrupt your partner while he or she is speaking. Be focused, interested and attentive. I knew a friend who used to interrupt to offer his wife advice each time she aired her grievances at work. A lot of men do this, and it isn't really their fault.

They are simply wired to fix everything since primitive times. A woman may simply want to talk her heart out to feel lighter. She may not necessarily be looking for advice, guidance, or suggestions. However, the man believes himself to be her knight in shining armor and starts offering immediate fix-it solutions. This can be true for women too at times. Resist the urge to offer solutions, and instead focus on listening to your partner.

After they are done speaking, you can figure out if they are soliciting advice. Don't jump the gun to throw in your two cents while they are still talking. Allow them to finish before offering advice.

Look at your partner while he or she is speaking and respond occasionally with a nod or verbal clues like "uh-huh", "I see" and "hmm." Set aside a daily talk time that is reserved only for you and your partner. It can be during breakfast or dinner or just before you go to bed. Respect the other person's need for talking or even staying silent. At times, the person may not want to talk, which is also alright. They may engage in a conversation when they feel more ready or energetic for it.

Even if you disagree with what he or she is saying, hang in for a while. Make honest and open communication your prime goal for a more rewarding and fulfilling relationship.

6. Pay Attention to the Overall Message

Reflect upon the message your partner conveyed via their words rather than simply catching a few words here and there. Check with them to know if you truly understand their feelings. You can do a check back like, "Honey, what I understand from what you are saying is" or "If I understand this correctly, then I think you are feeling...."

This tells your partner that you care about what they are saying, and are tuned in to their message. You are deeply invested in ensuring that you understand them correctly, and there's no scope for misunderstanding or miscommunication. Again, this helps you empathize with the other partner's perspective.

7. Appreciate Their Strengths by Overlooking Trivial Things

Each day make it a habit to inform your partner how much you admire them by saying something like, "I am thoroughly impressed by the way you handle people" or "You are a wonderful cook" or "You have an impeccable sense of style." It feels great to be appreciated, and sharing positive thoughts can have a pleasant influence on your relationship. If you are using this communication technique, ensure that the strengths you are listing are genuine. If not, your partner may get the feeling that you are being insincere in your praise. Be genuine, and point out specific strengths.

There will be some things about your partner, which will totally drive you nuts. If it's not something dangerous, destructive, unsafe, or unhealthy, learn to let go of these quirks. If they are perpetually misplacing their things or leaving wet towels on the bed, gently point it out to them without being accusatory. Overlook the person's pesky behavior, however annoying it may seem. Remember, it is a total of these quirks and strengths that make him or her unique.

8. Demonstrate Compassion and Respect

Demonstrate a sense of compassion for your partner's feelings. Once you've determined their feelings, it becomes easier to get yourself to accept how they are feeling. Learn to accept your anxiety, anger, and other emotions to develop handle conflicts or differences in a more empathetic manner. Be more mindful and accepting of your emotions.

Understand when people direct anger towards you, they are probably protecting their vulnerability and helplessness. Learn to detect the vulnerability behind what your partner is stating. Be more attentive to their needs, weak points, and sufferings.

It is natural to feel a sense of anger, hurt, guilt, and resentment towards your partner. It can be owing to a difference in opinion or frustration or as a result of your stress. Irrespective of the underlying emotion you are experiencing, respect should be the buzzword for any relationship. John Gottman, an authority on marriage and divorce states that couples who solve their fights swiftly and peacefully are those who use respect while fighting.

9. Be Specific About Your Requirements from Your Partner

One of the biggest mistakes couples makes is instead of focusing a conversation on what they want; they tend to focus their communication on what they don't want. Don't believe me? Each time you are talking to your partner, note what exactly the focus of the conversation is. Aren't you telling each other more of what you don't want or like rather than what you want from each other?

Please understand and highlight this if you want – your partner is not a mind-reader! I know couples who fight nineteen to a dozen because they are upset that the other person didn't understand what they wanted or what they were thinking. Be specific about your wants if you want your partner to do things for you.

Don't be focused on problems as a couple, focus on solutions instead. Avoid playing guessing games or trying to test your partner. Be clear and specific about your wants. This alone will save the relationship plenty of heartaches.

Chapter Two: Overcoming Challenges and Repairing Broken Trust

A relationship or marriage without problems, differences, and disagreements is an illusion. There are differences and disagreements galore in every intimate relationship. The only important consideration is how you resolve the disagreement to create a stronger bond. How do you get your partner to listen to you? How do you get them to change by communicating in the right manner? How do you move past disagreements and differences? How do you repair broken trust? How can you agree to disagree and be happy?

Tips To Get Your Partner to Listen To You

When one or even both partners don't listen to each other, your relationship may be in serious trouble. The lack of listening either on your part or your partner's side can lead to unaddressed issues, lack of understanding, or apathy, which can jeopardize your bond. Issues related to listening can be about their inability to listen or your way of delivering the message or both. Here are some tips for getting your partner to listen to you.

1. One of the biggest reasons why people switch off is because you may be speaking too long or taking a long time to communicate what you want. Long-winded or verbose messages often lose the main gist of what you are trying to say, thus making your partner warier of what you are trying to communicate. Stay to the point.

Similarly, many people have the habit of completely monopolizing or hijacking a conversation, while raring giving their partner a chance to speak. If you don't give your partner a chance to present their point of view or speak, there's little chance they are going to give you a patient hearing. Similarly, if you have a history of hurling threats, insults, abuses, and personal attacks, your partner will get defensive by switching off completely from the conversation. Don't say mean and disrespectful things if you want to be heard.

Also, stick to the point at hand. There are fewer chances of your partner listening to you if you are bringing all past issues, his or her family history, their dog's pedigree, and other unrelated personal attacks into the argument. If you want your partner to listen to you, stick only to the point at hand. When people realize you are trying to hit them hard by raking up past issues instead of resolving the current one, they immediately recoil and become defensive, even though they may be at fault.

2. Your partner is not likely to listen to you if you have a proven manipulation pattern in how you speak to them or get them to do things. They will tune out once they realize that you manipulate their feelings and emotions to have things go your way. Stop all manipulative communication tactics. Stick to saying what you really mean. Rather than saying, "If you really love me, you'll do this for me" or "if you don't do this for me, you don't love me" say something like, "I'd really be delighted if you did this for me." Don't threaten or emotionally blackmail your partner to get them to listen to you.

Some people have the habit of speaking to their partners in a patronizing, condescending, preachy, and lecturing manner. In such a scenario, partners will more often than not switch off from the lecture style conversation. Put your point across in a more conversational and non-accusatory manner. The more preachy and accusatory you make it, the higher will the chances of your partner switching off from the conversation. Stop lecturing and questioning, and try to adopt a more conversational, casual, and friendly approach to get the person to talk!

Don't play professor and FBI each time you attempt to have a conversation with your partner or even confront them.

3. Avoid using generalities such as "always", "never", "perpetually" and more, which can immediately cause your partner to switch off from the conversation simply because it doesn't sound realistic. When they realize that you are exaggerating things to prove your point or resorting to hyperbole to communicate an issue, they will act defensively. Remove these words from your conversation if you want to communicate effectively with your spouse.

4. Keep the timing right. Of course, you want to jump on your partner right away and talk to them about an issue that has been troubling you throughout the day the moment you see them back from work. However, pretty much like everything else, there is a right time for talking too.

Unless it is an urgent matter, avoid talking to your partner when they are tired, stressed, preoccupied with work or another activity, or sleepy. They may be deeply involved in an office project or watch television after an exhausting day at work. Ask them before initiating the conversation if this is a good time to talk to them. If they don't wish you talk right then, respect it instead of sulking.

Also, your partner will grow tired of conversations involving constant complaining, nagging, accusations, whining, or talking negatively about everything under the sun. Stay more positive in your conversations if you want your partner or anyone else to tune in more keenly.

5. The attention span of an average adult is merely 7 seconds, which means if you want your partner to listen to you, pause every once in a while to give them a break. Allow them to ask questions or clarify their understanding of what they've said. Let them refresh and process their thoughts. With a short attention span, people will invariably switch off if you keep talking without a break. For holding people's attention, pause or take breaks frequently.

Moving Past Differences and Disagreements

1. Be committed to managing disagreements positively. For people who are not very confrontational or argumentative y nature, it is easy to flee away from a disagreement. However, your relationship needs that you put these differences behind you to flourish and grow. Both you and your partner should be committed to handling disagreements healthily and positively.

I would highly recommend using positive language to manage differences and disagreements. If you can share your deepest feelings and emotions positively, that's a huge victory for the relationship, irrespective of your differences. One of the ways of using positive language is to try and minimize the usage of "you" and stick to more of "I" in its place. This way you put across your point as if it is your opinion rather than directly attacking your spouse.

For example, instead of saying something such as, "you never.... Say something along the lines of "I frequently feel...." It's a small shift that can make a huge difference in the manner in which a person receives what you are saying. It will help you put behind your differences and disagreements as a couple in a healthier manner than directly attacking the person.

2. Attack the differences instead of each other. Disagreements, arguments, and differences should be limited only to the points where you disagree with your partner. Some couples use small arguments or differences for more global attacks. Question their decision, action, thoughts, and behavior related to the disagreement rather than referring to them as a "horrible and evil person."

I know it is easier said than done. It isn't easy to think rationally or logically when you are fuming with rage. However, take a long, deep breath and remember that your partner and you are not two opposite warring sides. You both are in the same team and involved in the common cause of keeping your relationship intact. Focus on supporting each other even when you don't agree on some matters.

Don't remove your anger, stress, or exhaustion from each other. View the problematic disagreement as a common enemy, and tackle it together as a team. Talk about it together and work out a compromise that is beneficial for both.

3. Practice intentional communication. I have said this before and I'll say it again, your partner is not a clairvoyant or mind reader. You need to express your thoughts freely if you want them to know how you are feeling. Make it easier for them by giving them the information they need to know rather than expecting them to guess all the time. Attempting to read their minds or expecting them to read your mind is a recipe for disaster. Most disagreements can be resolved when you speak.

Open your heart and ears to listen to your partner in a non-judgmental manner. Look at things from both perspectives in case of differences. Maybe your partner does have a point where he or she comes from. Place yourself in their shoes and try to understand why they feel the way they do. Sometimes, it's impossible to understand where a person is coming from. Even in such a scenario, respect each other. Put away your phone, turn off the television and give them your full attention when they wish to talk. Hear your partner before judging them. It creates a more supportive and positive environment for resolving differences and conflicts.

4. Be alright with disagreements or differences as a couple. Learn to deal with your differences rather than letting them get the better of you. Some couples spend years attempting to change each other's opinions, values, thoughts, or beliefs. This isn't always possible because our disagreements are primarily rooted in our core fundamental values, personality, and opinion. Don't fight over these deeply rooted differences. You'll waste precious time and convert your relationship into a battleground.

What does one do in such a scenario? Simple, learn to accept each other as you are. As a couple, accept the fact that differences are an inevitable aspect of your relationship. They are similar to back or knee pain. You don't want back pain obviously! However, when you have it, you learn to cope with it. You develop strategies for managing the pain or overcoming it. Similarly, few people get into a relationship anticipating differences and disagreements. In an ideal world, they don't exist.

However, once we know there are differences, learn to manage them effectively. Some differences will remain unsolvable in a long-term relationship. You just have to communicate positively and learn to manage these differences as a couple. Learn to agree to disagree healthily as a couple for the overall good of your relationship. Keep your eyes on the bigger picture without allowing tiny differences to get in the way.

5. Sometimes offer help instead of whining to resolve differences and disagreements. For example, if your partner is working late, while you think they should be spending more time with you, ask if there's anything you can do to help them. Show concern and compliment them before telling them that you'd really like to spend more time with them. This will make them more open to listening to you rather than you getting into a "you are never home on time" or "you never spend time with me." It all depends on the way you frame it. If you put it across in a thoughtful, concerned, and understanding manner, your partner is more likely to listen to it and work on it.

Repairing Broken Trust

Broken trust can be related to infidelity, false promises, lies, and other major problems that wreak havoc in a relationship. The trust between the two partners is destroyed owing to the above scenarios. This doesn't mean that the bond cannot be salvaged. Rebuilding trust may require plenty of time and effort. Rebuilding trust can be a real challenge when it comes to saving the relationship. However, communicated and dealt with in the right manner, has the power to make your bond stronger and more intimate.

1. If you are the person who cheated, told lies, demonstrated errant behavior, etc., you have to go the extra mile to show your partner you've changed. You have to answer their questions, deal with their suspicions and generally be more open and forthcoming of details. They are bound to feel broken, hurt and angry. Avoid resorting to secrets and keeping things hidden. Make a conscious effort to involve your partner in all aspects of your life. Be more transparent, forthcoming, and straightforward.

2. The hurt partner should share their pain and talk about their feelings to the errant spouse.

This helps them relieve their pain rather than building pain, hurt, and resentment over the years. It isn't healthy to build and feel pent up pain. The partner who cheated must go out of the way to understand and empathize with their partner's pain. Show your partner that their feelings matter to you and that you are keen on contributing to their healing. Show empathy, concern, and thoughtfulness for your partner while they are getting over the hurt and pain.

3. Don't delay apologizing. Depending on what you've done to break your partner's trust, don't waste time when it comes to offering a sincere apology. Apologizing tends to diffuse tension within the relationship and assists with better communication. It can open the doors of meaningful conversation and communication, which may help you both, put the incident behind you. Delaying an apology once your partner knows everything will only make matters worse. Saying sorry makes you come across as more genuine and honest rather than offering lame justifications or explanations.

4. Let your partner talk openly about whether they've cheated on you or you've cheated on them. If your errant partner is describing what happened, allow them to speak rather than

judging and interrupting them. If you are the partner who has cheated, describe things as they happened and acknowledge how you've ended up hurting your spouse. This simple acknowledgment makes things a lot easier. It doesn't put the other person in an attack mode.

Though apologizing may seem unpleasant or challenging, it's necessary for the health of your relationship. Be open to answering questions they may have. Give straight and forthcoming answers rather than being evasive, which will only add to your partner's suspicion. Don't get defensive or make excuses for your deeds. It will only make matters worse. Appear genuinely remorseful. Apologizing has no value if you follow it up with justifications or blame your partner for it. Feelings of guilt and regret are hard to express. However, when you express them, it reveals your concern for genuinely attempting to work on the relationship.

5. Accept full responsibility for your actions and talk to your partner about what steps to plan to take to better the situation. Ask your partner what they require from your side to rebuild the trust. Do they have any specific needs that will help them trust you in the future or get over the pain? Your partner may closely monitor your

calls, emails, where you go, etc. in the future. Don't be defensive against these requests. It may make your partner even more suspicious. They may want to know more details about your affair.

Chapter Three: Apologies and Forgiveness

Funnily, apologizing can be the hardest and easiest thing to do, depending on how you approach it. It can be a huge relationship savior if you've done something terribly wrong to hurt your partner or an argument diffuser even if it isn't really your fault. Remember, it isn't always important to be right if you want a rewarding and fulfilling married life. Sometimes, hearing and being heard is the most important aspect of seeking or giving forgiveness. I know several relationships, which have toppled because of people's obsession to be right all the time. Sometimes, the bigger victory is in letting the other person believe that he or she is right even when they aren't.

Here are a few ways to communicate your apology to your partner in a thoughtful, meaningful, and genuine manner.

1. Don't use 'but' when you say sorry. Anything you add after 'but' seems like your defense or justification for doing something, which makes the apology appear insincere. When you are

apologizing, do it without any explanations and justification.

2. Never assume that your partner will forgive you. They have every right to not grant forgiveness, especially if you've broken their trust or hurt them deeply. Ask for forgiveness without expecting it to be birthright to be forgiven. You can never demand forgiveness. It is your partner's prerogative whether they forgive you or not. Don't hold any expectations about being immediately forgiven by your spouse. They may need more time to let the feeling sink in.

Forgiveness may take time, and may not be given instantly. You may not be able to control how the other person will react to your request for forgiveness. Give your partner the space and time he or she needs to heal and process what has happened. You may say sorry to the best of your ability or in the sincerest manner. However, how they react to it is completely their prerogative.

3. Never blame your partner for your actions and behavior when you are asking for forgiveness. Accept complete responsibility for the hurtful things you did and said without blaming anyone

for it. Also, express gratitude or thankfulness for your partner's patience in dealing with you. Don't take their forgiveness for granted or as a license to hurt them in the future. Be thankful that they have chosen to forgive you when you may not deserve it.

4. Pick your words carefully. Use gentle, honest, and soft words. Talk like you normally talk without sounding fake, contrived, or overly apologetic. It will make your apology comes across as insincere. If you are giving your partner an apology note, make it more personal and genuine by handwriting the note rather than buying a readymade card or apologizing via email or text. Sending a voicemail is probably more personal than sending a text message. Choose your medium and words carefully.

5. Avoid invalidating or dismissing your spouse's feelings by using words like, "if you felt hurt" or "if I hurt or offended you in any way." You are simply telling them that you don't think you've done anything wrong. However, if they felt offended (which seems like their fault), you are apologizing. It seems like they've got upset over a trivial issue and you are offering an apology only to pacify them.

At times, you should apologize even before your partner has communicated their hurt and regret. It makes your apology comes across as more proactive and genuine. Don't make your partner feel like he or she is not justified in feeling angry or hurt. Invalidating someone's feelings is a huge disservice to the act of apologizing.

6. Don't bring out past scorecards when you are apologizing. There is no need to bring out past pain, fights, hurt, regret and transgressions when you are apologizing. Nothing can be worse than "but you did this last year too" or "I am sorry about this but do you recall when you had done something similar two summers ago?" It shows your apology in a pathetic light, making it fake and forced.

7. Acknowledge your spouse's feelings. Even if you don't believe you did something wrong, it doesn't hurt to simply acknowledge your spouse's feelings. It may make your relationship stronger in the long run. Take time to listen and understand what has hurt or upset your partner instead of getting into the habit of offering an insincere, blanket apology for everything. If you apologize for everything, it will eventually lose its value.

Try to look at things from your partner's perspective even if you think you were not at fault. Take into account their feelings, emotions, thoughts, and perspectives on the issue. Try and empathize with your partner even when you don't necessarily agree with them. Show caring and understanding wherever possible, and attempt to offer a sincere apology if you realize you may have hurt their feelings.

8. Once you've apologized and dived into the heart of the matter, attempt to resolve issues by making a thoughtful change plan. For example, you can say something like, "from now on, I will consult you or talk to you before making a big purchase" or "I will do everything in my capacity to reorganize my schedule for spending more time with you and ensure that our relationship is given top priority.

Though you are apologizing here, you are also involving your partner in the plan of action or compromise here to show your commitment towards improving the situation for both. Making a clear plan of action reveals that you are committed and concerned about the relationship and each other's happiness. An apology backed by action sounds genuine and sincere, otherwise, it's nothing more than words. It will reveal to your partner that you truly mean what you say, and are concerned about improving the situation.

Forgiving Your Partner

Forgiveness is a process takes a lot of time and effort. You aren't inviting the other person to mistreat you in the future. Forgiveness is also not a sign of weakness. If anything, it takes a lot of strength and courage to forgive a person who has hurt you. Here are some ways to help you get rid of resentment and make your relationship stronger.

Having said that let me also reinforce the fact that some issues such as continued infidelity or instances of mental/physical abuse, addiction, etc. may not be forgivable. You may have to seek professional intervention or make a decision about whether you want to stay in the relationship.

1. Pour your feelings on paper. Write everything about what happened and how you felt about it. Putting everything down on paper is therapeutic. It will help you release your pent-up feelings, and heal faster. Release your feelings, and process them to avoid holding on to the pain for long. Once you express them in some form,

you'll feel less burdened by them. Write in detail about your spouse's actions and how they affected you. Write about your thoughts related to overcoming the pain and the process of forgiveness.

2. Take an inventory. This is one of my favorite tips when it comes to forgiveness. Make a list of your spouse's good qualities and all the good they've done for you. You'll soon realize in the process of making the list that he or she isn't really all bad. Which traits or characteristics of your partner like the most? Which are the instances where he or she has proven that they truly care about you? Make a list of all these positives, and you'll be surprised. Look at the list once in a few days. It will invariably bring about a shift in your thinking.

3. Don't see yourself as a victim, while also being kind towards yourself. Don't look back and feel sorry for yourself or view yourself as the wronged victim. Get rid of the "poor me" syndrome. Give yourself more credit than that. Bring about a shift in your thought process, where you aren't just the victim. For example, think about how every couple or relationship has its share of hits and misses, and this is probably

your time to struggle as a couple so your relationship comes out even stronger.

Changing the narrative can make all the difference. At the same time, forgiveness is not an event that can be conducted instantly. Don't hit yourself hard to get over the setbacks instantly. Your wounds may be raw, and they may take a while to heal. Be gentle and compassionate with yourself. It is important to forgive your spouse. However, it may not happen immediately, which is alright. It is fine to give the process of forgiveness and healing time until you feel ready to forgive and put the situation behind you.

4. Find a sense of serenity and peace with yourself. Sometimes forgiving a person and putting everything behind you can be intensely stressful. Use some type of stress management techniques to help you cope with the hurt and pain, and expedite the healing process. Walk, meditate, practice yoga, go for long walks, dance, swim, do kickboxing, cycle, do aerobics – just about anything that helps you find a sense of peace. Some of the meditation of physical activity will calm your senses down, and prevent angry thoughts from cascading.

5. Be empathetic. Empathy is the ability to work in another person's shoes. Try to understand where exactly your partner coming from. They may have had a different upbringing than you or they may have lived through different circumstances and experiences than you. This shouldn't be used to justify their actions. It just helps you gain an understanding of how or why they behaved in a particular way, which can lessen your hurt and increase compassion.

6. Talk to someone trusted other than your spouse. If you are finding it tough to get over your spouse's act or forgive him/her, seek professional intervention. Acknowledge your hurt and pain, and talk to a trusted friend or family member about it. Don't feel guilty for feeling hurt or angry. Try not to let irrational or illogical thoughts get the better of you. Appeal to your logical side rather than letting destructive emotions play havoc in your mind. You will feel much better when you release anger and irrational thoughts.

7. Avoid focusing on the negative and living in the past. Once you've decided to put something behind you, don't keep replaying it in your mind now and then. Don't let irrational beliefs occupy your mind. One of the most important things to

keep in mind about forgiveness is that it isn't just something we do for the other person but also ourselves. You hold on to the anger, pain, stress, and hurt – all of which affect you. When you forgive, you free yourself from all these negative emotions to let more positive thoughts and feelings occupy your mind.

Think about it like this. Everyone makes mistakes. If you keep holding on to past hurt or pain, you'll find it hard to accept even sincere apologies. You may find it challenging to feel positive about your partner or the relationship. When you make up your mind not to forgive your spouse, you hold on to plenty of anger, hurt, and pain. We feel much better when we don't have negative thoughts occupying our minds. It does as much harm to you (in fact much more) than it does to your spouse. Do you really deserve to have your mind occupied with negative emotions even when you aren't at fault or haven't done anything wrong? Again, forgiveness may not necessarily apply to everything. You may have your non-negotiators, which can be anything from physical abuse to drug addiction. However, if the matter is something that can be repaired, it may be worth it for helping you enjoy a more rewarding and fulfilling relationship.

Chapter Four: Communication for Avoiding Fights

There are several ways to communicate with your spouse without offending their feelings or increasing arguments. One can remain assertive and put their point across in a more non-offensive and effective manner by using a series of highly proven communication tactics. Though communication styles can vary, the ultimate goal should convey your point more convincingly and persuasively to avoid hurting the other person's feelings and to prevent any potential misunderstandings.

Here are some tips that will help you avoid fights or communicate without getting offended.

1. Know the Other Person's Perspective

Almost always, there are two sides to every story. Likewise, any disagreement has two distinct angles. It can simply be a matter of perspective. Your partner may be seeing things differently from you, and unless you are open to hearing their perspective, you won't know what they are thinking or how they are seeing things. Listen, and understand their perspective rather than staunchly believing that yours is the only right way of thinking.

Show genuine interest in understanding them even though you may not necessarily agree with them. Many times, we may not agree with what our spouse says or believes. However, it doesn't mean we shouldn't lend them a patient hearing or at least understand where they are coming from.

For example, your spouse may appear to be over-possessive, jealous, and suspicious about you all the time, which you may not agree with or accept. In your eyes, you've done nothing to trigger suspicion or possessiveness. However, the spouse may have been cheated in past relationships, and are therefore unable to get over the feeling. This may have made them increasingly jealous, possessive, and suspicious in all relationships. Of course, you don't have to live with your spouse's past baggage, and it can be highly annoying.

However, that doesn't mean you shouldn't show understanding or concern towards them. Understand where they are coming from even if you may not appreciate it. Grab opportunities to get them to talk, and listen to their perspectives. You may gain insights you hadn't otherwise considered. The explanation or flow of conversation may hold points that you had otherwise missed.

One of the guaranteed ways to avoid hurting others is putting yourself in their shoes. Imagine things from their perspective. How would you feel if you were in their place and he/she would talk to you the way you are talking to them? Wouldn't you be hurt and upset? Practice imagining or visualizing how the other person feels when you say or do certain hurtful things. Just because someone's opinion doesn't match yours, doesn't mean they are wrong.

2. Control Your Verbal and Non-Verbal Body Language

Be cautious with your honestly and straightforwardness at times. You want to be truthful and communicate your feelings, yes. However, truth should also be accompanied by compassion and kindness. Don't take potshots at their dreams or ideas. Even if you think something isn't going to work, tell them more kindly. For example, your spouse may come up with a business plan that you know isn't feasible in reality. Keep your words and actions in check.

Instead of making fun of the plan of their ideas, sit with them and talk to them about how it can be much better if they put in some time, effort, and thought into it. You want to be honest rather than mislead them, but you also want to do it in a manner that isn't hurtful. Don't grimace or use offensive/derogatory words. Never get personal or rake up past issues in the present argument.

Sometimes, the mere tone of your voice is enough to send people in another direction or convey your disappointment or disapproval. Unlike our words, the voice tone is more subconsciously guided. This means that our feelings, thoughts, and emotions are evident through the voice even though words can be manipulated in a certain manner. Try to talk with a more neutral tone if you don't want to communicate your feelings or wish you keep them in control.

Once you have already expressed your disagreement or disappointment verbally to your spouse, there is no need to back it up with non-verbal actions too. Once you've made your point, avoid repeating it or using other forms of communication to convey the same point once you've driven it home effectively.

It can only end up hurting your cause as constantly telling a person something potentially offensive makes them feel like you're accusing them and puts them on the defensive.

3. Construct Your Sentences as Opinions and Not Facts

When you are telling your spouse something that can be potentially offensive or hurtful, don't put it across as the ultimate gospel truth or fact! Facts work for people who have a more open and liberal perspective. However, it may seem accusatory or similar to personal attacks for people who are not open to understanding a different point of view. Don't force your perspective as the only truth. Avoid criticizing, demonizing, or condemning people.

Instead of using statements such as, "you are absolutely wrong", try something like, "I think you may not be right there." You are stating it as a perspective or opinion instead of brandishing judgments. You can also agree with their justification or perspective if the two are consistent. This reveals that your statement is not directly addressed to them in a hateful manner or to get back to them. Avoid exaggerating reality. Don't use words such as "never" or "always." In the heat of the moment, we use idioms and phrases that stretch the truth. Don't resort to hype roles, stick to honesty. Don't allow your emotions to speed up.

Take a deep breath and get a good grip on your emotions before you take off on your spouse. I know people, who in a bid to control or manage their emotions more effectively; take some time off to cool down before speaking to their partner. A cooling-off period ensures that you are not making the heat of the moment statements or accusations. You also more time to keep your body language and non-verbal clues in check.

4. Don't Take Disagreements Personally

Being honest and being right are two different things. You can be wrong and honest for all you know. Just because someone is stating their point honestly doesn't make them right. Similarly, you can be right, honest, and end up hurting your spouse's feelings. Be genuine about your perspective but if your spouse disagrees with it, don't take it personally. There may be a perspective or justification for their disagreement.

Resist the urge to transform their perspective to match yours. Just listen and absorb what they are trying to communicate. They have the right to their opinion and honesty just as you had a right to yours. Value your opinion, point of view, and perspective. Even if you don't disagree verbally or vociferously, remember your opinion is valid. You have as much right, to be honest about your perspective as the other person.

If you offer an honest perspective, and your spouse isn't open to hearing from you, pushing the issue will only make matters worse and create hurtful feelings. He or she may not be ready for agreeing with you. Avoid succumbing to the temptation of getting the other person to agree with everything you are saying. Sometimes, people should be allowed to make their mistakes. Also, if they don't agree with you, it doesn't make you wrong. It just means the person has a different perspective, which you shouldn't take too personally.

Tips for Diffusing Arguments with Your Partner

Arguments are an inescapable part of married life. If a couple says they never argue about anything, chances are they are lying. When two distinct individuals are involved, there are bound to be differences. There are heated discussions with people we truly care about or those we are close to. This is naturally true for our spouse too. Arguments may not be avoidable. However, not letting things snowball or get bigger is completely within our realm of control.

If you are drawn into a verbal altercation, use the following tips for defusing the argument and returning to a place of calmness and tranquility, where differences can be discussed more healthily and rationally.

1. Pick Your Battles

In a perfect world, all arguments will end with both parties agreeing to each other's perspective and moving away in a fulfilled and positive manner. However, the reality is far different than the perfect couple kingdom we dream of building. Differences don't automatically evaporate in thin air. The key to conflict management is learning to identify a lost cause. Pick your battles wisely. Know when it's not going to be worth it to put up a good fight.

Look at the overall good rather than holding on to your viewpoint in a stubborn manner. If budging slightly is going to save you time and plenty of heartaches, it may be worth it.

For instance, several happy and wise couples learn that there are plenty of topics that shouldn't be discussed between them such as politics or relatives (potentially acrimonious topics). Understand that there are topics, where differences will always exist. It is sensible to avoid these topics.

2. Calm Down

Even minor arguments can snowball into large issues if they aren't tackled or nipped in the bud. If both you and your spouse let a minor issue blow up into something huge by letting your emotions get the better of you, there's going to be nothing but fights. Damaging words can cause irreparable damage to the relationship, which you or your spouse may later regret. Avoid letting your emotions get the better of you in any situation, and stay as calm as possible.

Practice anger management hacks such as deep breathing or counting up to 20. Take a break from the argument if you think it is on the verge of becoming more intense. Go for a walk, give it some time, and come back with a fresh perspective. Avoid all this by being calm. Each time you find your anger rising, do something relaxing, therapeutic, and stress-busting before going back into the discussion. It won't just reduce your anger but also give you greater clarity of perspective. Sometimes, when you give it time, you'll realize that you hadn't really seen it from the other person's point of view.

3. Stick Only To the Topic

A healthy argument is always to the point and non-personal. There's no place for raking up past issues or hitting below the belt on matters that are totally unconnected or irrelevant to the topic of argument. If you use personal insults or hit at the other person's character, it reveals a lot about yours. When we are seething with rage, it is easy to lose perspective or broaden the scope of our fight. The dispute or difference becomes a scope to settle scores or get even with your partner by using a variety of attacks.

This annoyance invariably includes all topics under the sun, including unfortunate personal attacks, which make matters worse. For example, you may start fighting about the fact that it is always you who is doing all household chores, while your partner watches television or plays virtual games. This doesn't mean you can tell him or her about how everyone in his or her family is lazy, low on ambition, and good for nothing. They may in return be shocked about how you are belittling their family and may say it to you.

To which, you will go on to reply that exactly 6 days, an hour and 36 seconds ago, he or she had said demeaning things about your family too. What you are doing is using a real current issue (not contributing towards household chores) for settling earlier scores. This doesn't resolve your current issue and makes past grudges even worse. Don't use a small argument about doing the laundry as a full-blown excuse for lashing out at your better half's character.

If you must squabble, keep it related to the issue at hand. Focus on the present issue rather than playing 'ten weeks ago you did so and so now I am getting even' game. This will lead to more hurt and pain, and the original matter remains unresolved. Focus on the issue at hand, and work out a middle way to tackle the conflict so you arrive at a more peaceful outcome. The more you and your spouse stick to specific details of an issue, the higher are your chances of resolving it more peacefully.

4. Watch Your Body Language, Tone, and Mannerisms

Hurtful and destructive confrontations comprise a bunch of painful and hurting insults that are hurled back and forth. Shouting at the top of your voice, displaying aggressiveness through body language, keeping a more standoffish stance, raising your tone and more are all signs of harshness. Sometimes, even without noticing or knowing if we come across as highly hostile.

Of course, you can see yourself in the mirror otherwise you'll know how hostile you look. Sometimes, while talking a person will slowly raise their tone unknowingly and demonstrate their rage-filled feelings! Speak in a more gentle, calm, polite, and neutral manner. This will make you come across as more assertive, and people will listen to you. Rather than screaming and yelling, talk to people in a more assertive, calm, and confident tone. Irrespective of the nature of the discussion, keeping a friendly disposition and attitude will ensure that the conflict doesn't escalate.

5. Accept Your Differences

In an ideal world, all arguments will end with both partners settling their differences and agreeing with each other's perspective, and walking away into the sunset holding hands. Reality and expectations are diverse worlds though. For god's sake, you are a couple not a pair of Siamese twins. Have you ever wondered how boring life will be if your spouse is exactly like you? There will be differences. However, these differences are the basis of making your relationship more exciting.

It's a good complement when you and your spouse combine forces to create a stellar relationship. Spouses needn't always think or be alike. Their differences can be a good complement to each other. Married life and communication become easier once you accept that there will be differences, and consciously work on these differences.

You and your spouse may have grown up in different environments with a different set of values and upbringing, which may have led to the development of a unique personality or beliefs. Don't get into a relationship with the notion that just because you both are a couple; you should be alike in all aspects.

Yes, you may have to be on the same thought process when it comes to joint decisions, say raising children, managing the house, and taking care of finances. However, it isn't necessary to be alike in everything. Learn to respect and celebrate each other's differences to enjoy a happier and more fulfilling relationship.

Chapter Five: Create or Re-Create Intimacy -Ways to Charm Your Partner and Get Them to Be Responsive To You and Like You More

Do you get the feeling that your partner doesn't show much interest in you off late? Has the intimacy between the two of you reduced considerably? When people say, all relationships have a shelf life of romance and intimacy after which it starts going downhill; I want to laugh out loud. Of course, things may get boring when you see the person day in and day out, and function on a routine.

However, that shouldn't stop you from continuing the honeymoon. When people say, it isn't working, what they really mean is they aren't working hard enough to make it work. Nothing works on its own – we have to make it work. There are lots of things that you can do to ignite the passion in your married life or add spice to it. Here are a few sizzling tips to recreate or create intimacy in your relationship, get your partner to adore you, and get them to be more responsive to your needs and desires.

1. Get Out of the House

Find your passion, and get out of the house to take some time for yourself and your hobbies. It will help your partner value you, even more, when he or she realizes that you have a life and passion of your own. It's necessary to be available at home all the time even if you are a stay at home parent or homemaker!

Find creative activities, join a reading club, volunteer towards charitable causes, sign-up for cooking class, learn a unique form of dancing or martial arts – there's so much to explore. Being a little less available will make your spouse look forward to seeing you or spending time with you, contrary to when you are with each other all the time, and nagging each other. You can also ask your spouse to join you for these activities occasionally. However, the main objective is to have a life of your own, distinct from your time and life a

Build friendships outside the relationship. Exchange notes and stories with friends and enjoy novel experiences to make your time away from your spouse interesting. Time apart is one of the major reasons for the success of any relationship. Owing to the time apart, you cherish your time together. Then there are romantic conversations over the phone. Though your relationship happens to be your primary relationship, it doesn't have to be the only one. Nurture and foster other relationships too to stay off each other's back for a while.

2. Pay Compliments and Don't Forget To Demonstrate Gratitude

During the dating phase, couples praise everything from each other's kerchiefs to 'your cute crooked tooth' to the way your tummy moves when you laugh. However, come long-term relationships or marriage, and we believe there's no need to tell the person that we love them or adore certain things about them because they already know or you've already won them over so then there's no challenge in it or fun in the chase. The real chase for keeping a relationship happy and fulfilled in the long term begins once you are married.

One of the most powerful ingredients for a super successful relationship is to pay sincere and meaningful compliments to your partner. Also, avoid taking everything they do for you for granted. Keep an attitude of gratitude if you want to enjoy a rewarding long-term relationship. Appreciate and thank your spouse for little things like packing your lunch, cooking your favorite meal, or getting your favorite ice-cream. Appreciate the thoughtfulness behind these small acts.

3. Maintain Passion and Intimacy

Intimacy isn't something that is restricted to the bedroom. Passion and intimacy is a state of mind that can just flow if you both make the right effort. It can be anything from sending naughty texts to your spouse in the middle of a busy workday or leaving little love/passion notes about what you to do to you in the bedroom. Think about aphrodisiacs such as a walk under the stars on a beach holding hands (and ending with a passionate kiss) or a weekend alone in a more secluded place.

Don't limit your passion or intimacy strategies to be defined by what others consider normal or acceptable. You may want to have sex four times a day, and as long as your spouse is alright with it, go for it! Know that over some time, priorities in a relationship can change. However, that doesn't make it any less interesting or exciting.

Sex isn't the only measure of intimacy. It can also include cuddling over a shared mug of hot chocolate while catching your favorite movie. Intimacy is also conversations, kissing, and cuddling.

4. Invest in Your Bond

Isn't it funny how we expect returns everywhere else only after investing and yet largely ignore investing in our relationship while still expecting it to reap rich rewards? Pretty much like everything else in life, you need to invest in your relationship to reignite the spark, make it sexy and enjoy a fulfilling relationship.

I know friends who plan sexy and intimate date nights or go for overnighters while leaving the children with a family member or babysitter. Then there are adult games that can spice up these overnighters for you and your spouse to reconnect intimately with each other, and create memorable moments.

Read a book together, sign up for a relationship retreat, try an online course together, and be committed to strengthening your relationship to bring back the spark. You must be committed to the process of bringing back the spark or reconnecting with your spouse before working out a plan to keep working on it periodically. How about a couple of massage or spa treatment once in a while?

5. Be Compassionate

We have a tendency to take advantage of or take for granted the people we love. This is probably because we think we can get away. Take, for example, you have a bad day at work and get yelled at by your boss. Once you get home, you take it out on your spouse because you have no one else to vent it out on, and your spouse will probably tolerate it more than anyone else would.

A healthier way to go about this would be asking yourself if your spouse is really at fault for what happened in the office. Some relationship counselors also recommend asking yourself at the beginning of each day what they can do to make their partner happy. It makes sense to put your best foot forward for the person you love, right?

In a happy bond and relationship, both the partners make an effort to please one another. You may have to sit through long, boring baseball games or watching soppy romantic flicks, talking about virtual gaming strategies, and visiting archeological sites when you'd be on a beach. Don't focus on your needs all the time.

6. Don't Leave Any Scope for Misunderstanding

One of the best ways to keep the charm in your relationship alive and get your partner to like you is by eliminating all potential misunderstandings through open communication channels. It is truly astounding how many relationships are destroyed and the spark is killed because both the partners are simply not talking to each other.

Let us consider a scenario for example. Jim and Rose (a married couple) are at the Jim office party to celebrate a huge milestone accomplished by the organization. Jim had a huge role in accomplishing the milestone and is predictably very popular with his managers and co-workers. As soon as Jim and Rose enter the party, Jim is surrounded by a bunch of co-workers congratulating and hailing his efforts. Since Jim is affable, friendly, and congenial by nature, women also find him nice and easy to talk to.

In the entire process, Rose feels ignored and left on her own! She thinks Jim is busy flirting and cracking jokes with his female co-workers while she is left to figure out things on her own. In her mind, Rose feels let down by Jim. In his mind, Jim is relaxed thinking Rose understands everything and is enjoying meeting new people on her. He thinks he is just being nice and friendly while cracking insider office jokes with his female co-workers. Rose doesn't communicate her displeasure to Jim straightaway. Instead, she sulks, keeps mum, and reveals her anger through her body language.

Jim doesn't understand why Rose is sulking when she should be having a good time at the party and should be proud of him. Rose, on the other hand, is upset about not being given enough attention by Jim. Thus, there is a mismatch of understanding and how the two partners perceive the same situation. When Jim tries inquiring on their way home what was bothering Rose throughout the party and why she was sulking, she snaps at him for not understanding.

This makes Jim all the more annoyed when in his mind he hasn't done anything wrong at all. He accuses Rose of being insecure, jealous, unreasonable, and possessive, which escalates the misunderstanding even further. Wouldn't it have been less complicated if they two had just spoken about each of them felt rather than playing guessing games or expecting the other person to read their mind?

If you really want to ignite the passion or charm in your long-term relationship or marriage, get into the habit of talking to your spouse and telling them exactly how you feel. There will be fewer conflicts, lower unpleasant situations, and much more loving moments once you learn to connect by talking. Get your spouse to like you more by talking about what is bothering you rather than letting the issue simmer over a while.

7. Don't Underestimate the Power of Touch

You don't have to jump on each other and have frenzied sex each time you are together. There are small ways through which you can build intimacy by holding hands, hugging your spouse, or kissing them on their forehead. How about giving them a relaxed and de-stressing massage?

Physical affection is important when it comes to keeping the spark alive, and it can be revealed through multiple ways than just going on an endless romp session. Even when a relationship is in trouble, these physical gestures of affection can help a relationship pull through. It shows both the partners that they are desired, loved, and wanted – something that keeps the relationship alive.

Touch your spouse when they least expect it. For example, wrapping your arms around him or her when he or she is cooking in the kitchen! Or gently massaging their head when they are tired and about to go to bed. These are small gestures that demonstrate your love and care for the other person.

8. Try New Things Together

One of the biggest ingredients of a successful relationship is the novelty factor. Keep the spark in your long-term relationship or marriage alive by doing new and exciting things as a couple. This will help you retain the freshness in your bond rather than letting mundane everyday life take over. Do new, fresh and exciting things together as a couple. It can be anything from skydiving to a backpacking trip in Asia to taking a class together. You may want to learn scuba diving together or play tennis every weekend. I knew a couple who in a bid to add freshness to their marriage or long-term relationship took a cooking class together. And boy did it work!

Pick up anything that offers a break from the usual routine, and gives you both something exciting to bond over. It can be as simple as exploring a genre of film you've never watched before. Adventure activities or sports can get your collective blood pumping, which can lead to a feeling of exhilaration and arousal that can lead to great sex and a bunch of romantic moments. You'll feel more attracted to your partner and driven by the desire to spend more time with them.

Conclusion

Thank you for downloading this book.

I genuinely hope it has offered you multiple strategies about communicating with your spouse to lay the foundation of a lasting, happy, and fulfilling relationship.

How should you talk to your spouse in a manner that they listen to? How should you resolve issues and get over your differences to live a more harmonious life?

The objective of the book is to help you set the tone of a long-lasting, happy, and fulfilling relationship, where both the spouses have communicated each other's needs, expectations, and wishes. Communication is the key to building a solid, rewarding, and lasting relationship.

The next step is to start using the strategies mentioned in the book right away. Start communicating with your partner in a meaningful way, do tiny things that increase the bond of communication between you and your spouse, and be committed to the pursuit of overcoming differences. If you've just had a challenging situation in the relationship, it may not improve immediately. It may be a slow process that needs more time, effort, and attention to gradually grow into a strong and indestructible bond.

Allow the relationship to blossom by contributing in your tiny ways to make your spouse feel special. Chalk out an arrangement beforehand about tackling conflicts and disagreements. Listen, and think about the other person while attempting to resolve differences. Keep an open communication and objective mindset approach.

Finally, if you enjoyed reading the book, please take the time to share your views by posting a review of Amazon. It'd be greatly appreciated!

CPSIA information can be obtained
at www.ICGtesting.com
Printed in the USA
LVHW060838280221
679537LV00054B/62